GARBAGE TRUCKS

by Amanda Doering Tourville
illustrated by Zachary Trover

Content Consultant:
Paul M. Goodrum, PE, PhD, Associate Professor
Department of Civil Engineering, University of Kentucky

magic
wagon

visit us at www.abdopublishing.com

Published by Magic Wagon, a division of the ABDO Group, 8000 West 78th Street, Edina, Minnesota, 55439. Copyright © 2009 by Abdo Consulting Group, Inc. International copyrights reserved in all countries. All rights reserved. No part of this book may be reproduced in any form without written permission from the publisher.

Looking Glass Library™ is a trademark and logo of Magic Wagon.

Printed in the United States.

Text by Amanda Doering Tourville
Illustrations by Zachary Trover
Edited by Patricia Stockland
Cover and interior design by Emily Love

Library of Congress Cataloging-in-Publication Data
Tourville, Amanda Doering, 1980-
  Garbage trucks / by Amanda Doering Tourville ; illustrated by Zachary Trover.
     p. cm. — (Mighty machines)
  Includes bibliographical references and index.
  ISBN 978-1-60270-625-5
  1. Refuse collection vehicles—Juvenile literature. I. Trover, Zachary, ill. II. Title.
  TD794.T68 2009
  628.4'42—dc22
                    2008036001

Table of Contents

What Is a Garbage Truck?

A garbage truck picks up trash from neighborhoods and businesses. It hauls the trash to landfills and recycling plants. Different trucks pick up waste in different ways.

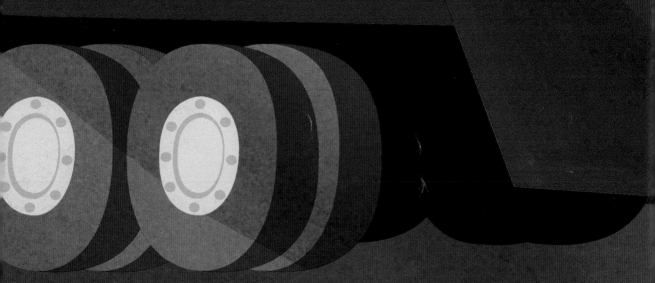

Parts of Garbage Trucks

Garbage trucks have a hopper, or bin, to hold the trash. Garbage is loaded into the hopper by people or other machines. The hopper opening is on the top of the truck, on the side of the truck, or in the rear of the truck.

Front-loading and side-loading garbage trucks have lifting arms. These arms lift garbage containers and dump the trash into the hopper. After the garbage is dumped, the arms set the container back down on the ground.

8

Rear-loading garbage trucks may have a tipping bar on the rear of the truck. A garbage collector places the garbage container on the tipping bar and pulls a lever. The bar lifts the containers to dump the trash.

Side-loading garbage trucks have small lifting arms.
They pick up smaller containers.

A compaction system is inside the hopper. This system presses the garbage to make it smaller. This makes room for more garbage.

Different trucks compact the garbage differently. Most front-loading trucks use a large blade that sweeps the trash to the back of the truck. A rear-loading truck has a moving wall that pushes garbage to the front of the truck. The large blades and moving walls are powered by hydraulic arms.

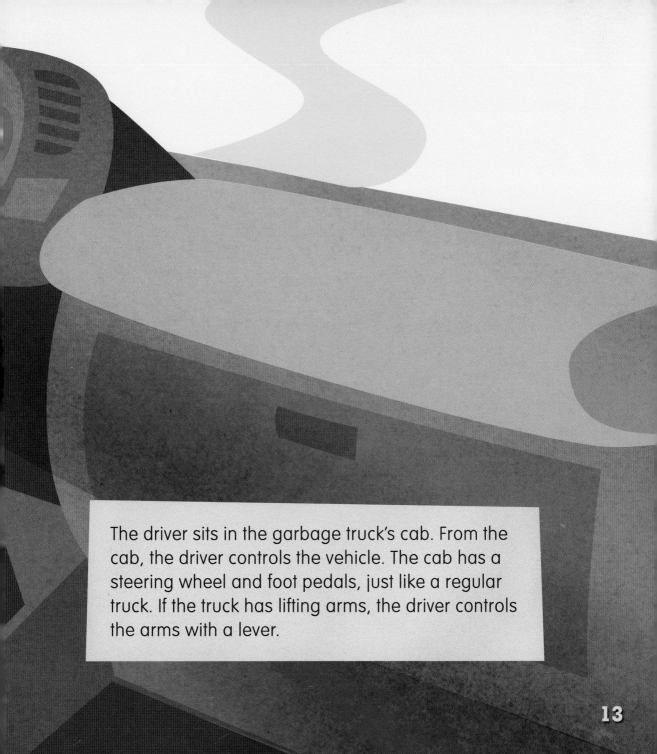

The driver sits in the garbage truck's cab. From the cab, the driver controls the vehicle. The cab has a steering wheel and foot pedals, just like a regular truck. If the truck has lifting arms, the driver controls the arms with a lever.

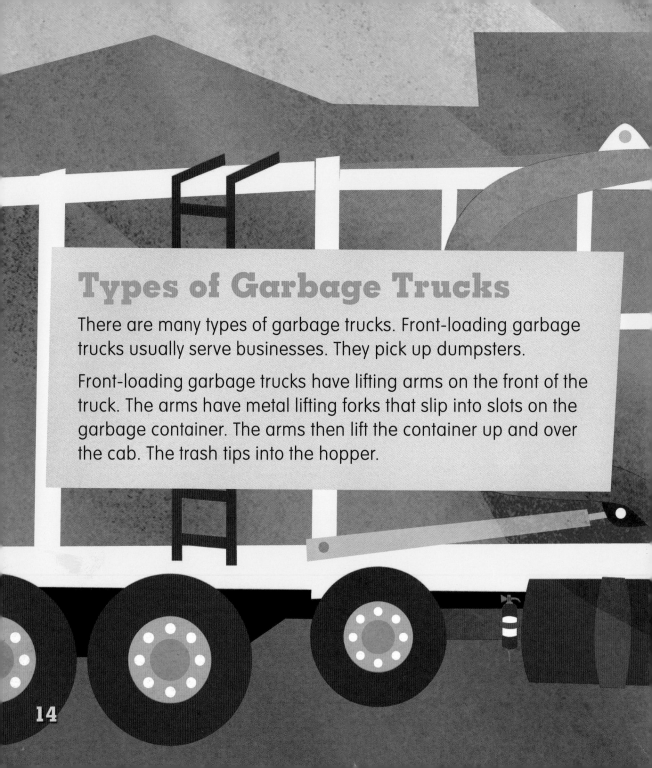

Types of Garbage Trucks

There are many types of garbage trucks. Front-loading garbage trucks usually serve businesses. They pick up dumpsters.

Front-loading garbage trucks have lifting arms on the front of the truck. The arms have metal lifting forks that slip into slots on the garbage container. The arms then lift the container up and over the cab. The trash tips into the hopper.

15

Side-loading garbage trucks are mostly used in neighborhoods. The opening is on the side of the vehicle, and the lifting arms are smaller than the front-loader. The arms lift the container and dump the trash into the truck.

Rear-loading garbage trucks are also used in neighborhoods. A garbage collector hooks the garbage containers to the tipping bar. The collector pulls a lever, and the bar lifts the containers to dump the garbage.

If the truck does not have a tipping bar, the garbage collector will throw the bags of trash into the hopper.

19

Roll-off garbage trucks serve construction sites and places with large amounts of trash. The large bin of a roll-off truck slides down a ramp. The bin stays at the site. When the bin is full, the truck comes back. The bin is rolled back onto the truck. The bin is then dumped at a disposal site.

21

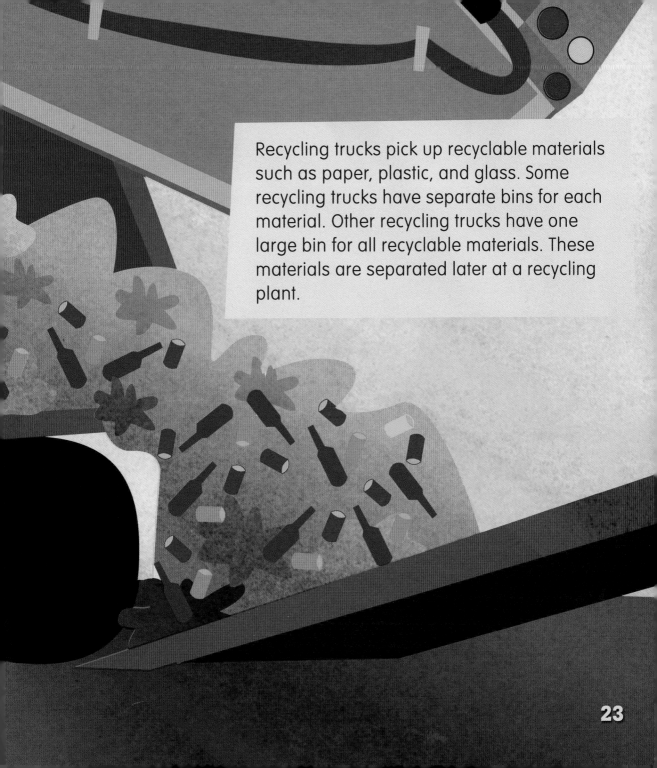

Recycling trucks pick up recyclable materials such as paper, plastic, and glass. Some recycling trucks have separate bins for each material. Other recycling trucks have one large bin for all recyclable materials. These materials are separated later at a recycling plant.

Where Are Garbage Trucks Used?

Garbage trucks are used wherever people live and work. People who live in large cities and those in the country need their trash picked up. Businesses and construction sites rely on garbage trucks to take their trash away, too.

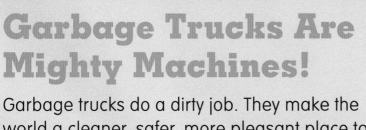

Garbage Trucks Are Mighty Machines!

Garbage trucks do a dirty job. They make the world a cleaner, safer, more pleasant place to live. Garbage trucks are mighty machines!

Garbage Truck Parts

Front-loading Garbage Truck

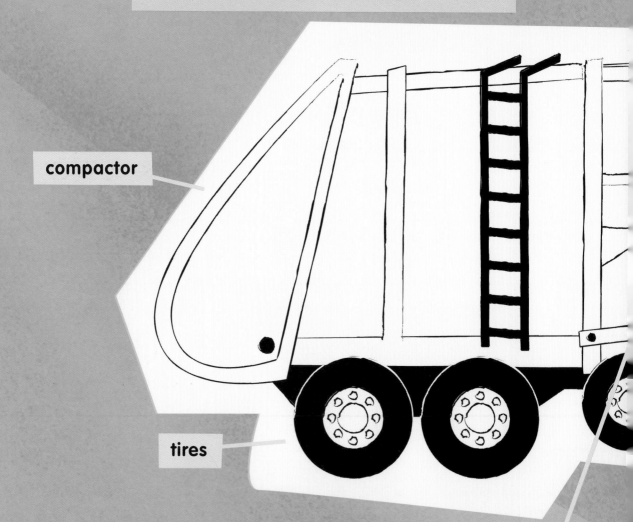

compactor

tires

hydraulic arm

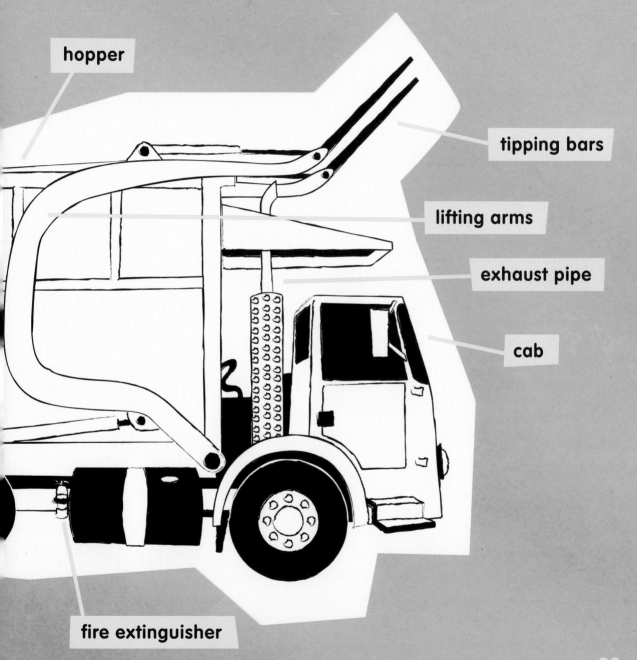

hopper

tipping bars

lifting arms

exhaust pipe

cab

fire extinguisher

29

Fun Facts

○ In Great Britain, garbage trucks are called dustbin lorries.

○ The first garbage vehicles were not trucks. Garbage was dumped into carts or wagons pulled by donkeys or horses.

○ When the truck is full, the garbage is taken to a holding area, landfill, or recycling plant.

○ The first garbage trucks were made in the 1920s. These trucks had open tops, which allowed garbage to blow out. They also let out the rotting-garbage smell. Garbage trucks were soon made with covers.

○ The United States generates about 250 million tons (227 million metric tons) of waste each year.

○ In 2009, there were approximately 136,000 garbage trucks and 31,000 recycling trucks in use in the United States.

○ Engineers are working on a new fuel for garbage trucks. The fuel is made from natural gas given off by landfills.

Glossary

compaction—pressing together to make smaller.

construction—the act of building or making something.

dumpster—a large trash container.

hydraulic—operated or moved by liquid.

landfill—an area where garbage is buried.

recycling—making new items from old items.

Web Sites

To learn more about garbage trucks, visit ABDO Group online at **www.abdopublishing.com**. Web sites about garbage trucks are featured on our Book Links page. These links are routinely monitored and updated to provide the most current information available.

Index